Leviathan

poems by

Chris Bullard

Finishing Line Press
Georgetown, Kentucky

Leviathan

Copyright © 2016 by Chris Bullard
ISBN 978-1-944251-66-6 First Edition
All rights reserved under International and Pan-American Copyright Conventions. No part of this book may be reproduced in any manner whatsoever without written permission from the publisher, except in the case of brief quotations embodied in critical articles and reviews.

ACKNOWLEDGMENTS

Editor: Christen Kincaid

Cover Art: Odilon Redon

Author Photo: Jan Bullard

Cover Design: Elizabeth Maines

Printed in the USA on acid-free paper.
Order online: www.finishinglinepress.com
 also available on amazon.com

Author inquiries and mail orders:
Finishing Line Press
P. O. Box 1626
Georgetown, Kentucky 40324
U. S. A.

Table of Contents

The Four Temperaments 1

Phase Book for Pessoa 5

Cruise Control 6

Neil deGrasse Tyson 7

Gramps 8

Land/Fill 9

Medusa 10

As Far as the Eye Can Kill 11

Leviathan 12

For Jan

The Four Temperaments

Spirits

The dry clouds clamored for a jigger
of lightning, but the pluvial bartender
was otherwise engaged. I could use
a fizz myself, this being a bicarbonate
sort of day with muricate words stuck
in the spatial blue muck. Pour me

Gin is like someone driving around
looking for trouble. Today the street
is full of lapses. Just saying, for example,
this puddle of sun anyone could fall.

Entering the watershed
I was not ashamed
though it was wet underneath.

Tip your head back and try not to choke.

Straight, No Chaser

We went heat-seeking in the darkness.
Novel that.
How sweetly structures burn.
Rinse and repeat.
Always bear in mind that flesh is a poor reactant.
Reading you 4 before.
The explosion pasted shadows on the walls.
Roger and out.

I am the scalpel in the precise hand of Dr. Gross.
I am Old Sparky blowing smoke on your synapses.
I am your brown-eyed girl sexting her step-daddy.
I am the bouquet burning on the stove.

A field, a ditch, the dry emblements of the body
flame.

Wine Cooler

O wild
cemetery man with a blower on his back
the dead billowing leaves.
The air saturate.

A libation, please.
Let's talk lovers
while I brush ash from your lapels.

Fewer pollinators despite the proliferation of private
gardens knock-out roses boxwood scented paths
water features packaged seed the sky almost opaque
with dandelion fluff.

ombre portate da la detta briga

The poet's orgasm is never described overtly says the critic.
A beech thrust from Whitman's tomb.

Rolling Rock

Actuarially absent in the statistical
present unaccounted for
by the expanded notation of billions:
I sperm ova ova ova sperm *ad infinitum*

a few dots stop
moving & shuffle off the sarcous papier mache.
The naming algorithm shifts into oracular indefiniteness.

Both here and not
among the missing grief
is a popular earworm
revolving it all.

There is a place in the ashlar dressed for you.
You will stay come to it.
Shoulder to shoulder tied to the sun.

Phrase Book for Pessoa

The pen of my dream lies on the desk of my office.
Waiter, I desire a mirror for myself and the others.
Yes, I would like more dark spots on my yellow bananas.
Excuse me, but this destiny is full.
Do you mind if I don't join you? I prefer to exist.
Please, what direction is the district of beauty?
You will need to wear a hat because the sun is so indefinite.
Thank you for these ghostly flowers of thought. They're my favorite.
Have we met before? I also was not there last year.
I am not I, but why do you suppose me to be you?

Cruise Control

Under the substantial
emptiness, the car skitters,
wheels orbiting like
dilated flying saucer
eyes dizzy with smeary
roadside colors, possibly
foam flower, possibly
chicory, aster, wild
carrot, natural remains
blurred at this speed,
smothered by the ledge
of sumac, materiality
scattered like the scree
humped on the linear
gestalt, as the make
and model travels
on its oblique errand
so not to arrive, gas
sucking the immediate
air, sealed coupe body
disengaged from all
words providing entry
or termination, dumb
to the residual silence
while held suspended
in the mad balancing
of agreed prepositional
dimensions: to/from,
above/below, in/on
like a machine Buddha
natant with wisdom.

Neil deGrasse Tyson

tells me creation is full of hadrons
and Higgs bosons so charmingly shy
they could show up with wide little eyes
under the foliage in a PBS wildlife special
although they're faster—zipping in and out
of existence until your left hemisphere
captures them in its personal cloud chamber
where you only know them because they interact
sending each other off at crazy angles
or maybe you might catch them somewhere
interesting in space/time: a star igniting
or even the Big Bang. Singly, yet ready
to combine with others, like words they
keep popping out of the background nothing.

Gramps

backed us   from the dinner table
puffing   dentures past lips
click-clacking   false choppers
like a machine gun   strafing jungle.

Hard-edged predator   age an eon
said he'd snatch   our noses   float them
as trophies   in his bedside water glass
where he stashed   that removable grin.

We held ears against   their chatter
but images of blades   gnawed
through dreams   slivering   souls
of school pals   into sacrifice

for the old man   for all old men
the invincible teeth   striding away.

Land/Fill

Yellow crawlers/on the trash mountain/
gulls rising from/the roiled aftermath/like winged steam/
sandwich wrappers/and hamburger cartons/
fluttering/in moth motions.

The dreaming engines/grind/
shifting the garbage/onto more garbage/
ravenous/
for more stuff/to stuff down.

This is our faith/
whatever we shovel/into this ninth circle/
is transformed/not choked on.

A mass requiring/even more mass,
what you bury/pulls you under/
tucks you next to its tumorous corpse.

Medusa

The male gaze uncovers her;

allowed an instant of appreciation

sees:
eyes brilliant as Catherine windows
skin like the moon behind high clouds
an extravagant animality of coiffure

while behind her waves curl without completion

and stiffens
possessed by the certainty
of possession.

Worshipfully affixed
his longing as immortal as marble,
how could the unloved lover leave
always knowing   this knowing?

As Far as the Eye Can Kill

The eyes scythe
the insurgent landscape
clear-cutting the extravagant images
and shifting subtle chromatics

bundling a view of the world
down the optic nerve
into the grey matter industrial park
where the factory mind

processes the gestalt
into visual plywood,
manufacturing a billboard narrative
of the world without complexity

this sensible whole
where you live seeing postcards.

Leviathan

I.

I swam in the cold aquamarine light.

II.

The beast's great mouth closed over me.

III.

I could not see, yet I was not blind
I soaked in a tide of brine and acid.
My nose closed down from the stench of digestion.
The resounding heartbeat drowned out all other sounds.
Taste, too, shut off.
My tongue was an amazed idiot declaring that the world had turned to salt.
Only touch communicated.
It allowed me to find the fish and seaweed scattered like fallen manna across this interior beach.
I strolled through the belly with the ease of one walking the rolling hills in summer darkness.
When I tired, my fingers felt for a place to fit my body.
I bent to the beast and laid myself upon his flesh.

IV.

The beast swept up fragments from the ocean.

A grab bag of parts drifted in his belly.

Wreckage rubbed along my leg as though my dog were welcoming me home:

planking and spars, hemp rope trailing like the tentacles of an octopus, half-awake fish, startled by my touch, smashed furniture with brass hinges, a bridle of kelp, canvas slick as skin, an oar, a bottle, something entangled in clothing - I shoved it away.

Aucune autre âme n'aurait assez de force, — force de désespoir ! — pour la supporter, — pour être protégée et aimée par lui.

I pushed away all reminders.

V.

The old fracture between sleep and consciousness did not exist.

Walk/eat/shit/walk/eat/shit/walk/eat/shit

(When I paused and oblivion extinguished my flickering anxiety, was this sleep?)

I moved again.

(Had an hour passed? A century? Could I drift backwards into time?)

Il en veut, mon esprit!

I tried to impose a narrative on my actions, but my familiar language, its construction of tenses, its sequences, the words that I had used daily, were useless. Those words had been a link to objectivity. This no longer existed.

(What word could describe my exile?)

(What word could describe this loss of my physical self, this reliance on another's body?)

Words had come to my tongue as easily as oxygen combines with hydrogen, but in the belly I was silent.

VI.

I do not remember my dreams.

Je m'habituai à l'hallucination simple:

(If I dreamed, was it of this place?
Did I dream of myself or of the beast?
Did I dream of myself as the whale or was I the beast's dream of itself?)

Without my senses, I had no proof of my own existence.

In a dark room a mirror has no use.

(Was I more interesting to myself doing nothing than doing something?)

VII.

The loss of my body in this unfamiliar body concentrated the self that remained.

My mind described what was not describable, observed what did not exist, imagined more than what its senses told it.

Le Bonheur était ma fatalité…

Those who lose their sight are said to enjoy a compensatory increase in their other senses.

This beast was all of my senses.

VIII.

Under the palm

        the sticky walls

stench of fish in the nostrils damp

        salt on the searching tongue

hunger the beast rises breaches

        I fall to my length

muscle against muscle

        skin sensing

the circuiting blood beneath

        concavity of form

who would absorb me

        who would take me

into this almost exhaustion

this almost release

IX.

Quelle bête faut-il adorer?

The beast carries me through the waters of this world.

He is my strength and my faith.

I am nourished in his body.

(The beast has confined me in his flesh.)

He is my unseen jailer.

(He is my darkness.)

He is a god;

(A failed god.)

I am more powerful because I live through him.

(He is my limit, the border to my thoughts.)

I am his companion.

(He is my madness.)

X.

No messages from the god; no decipherable word.

The body continues: mechanical, rhythmic.

(Sounds: are they the components of a language?
Perhaps the lack of communication is itself communication of a higher order.)

I do not attempt to speak.

(How should the parasite address his host?
What means of expression could insinuate itself through those hierarchic layers of skin and muscle to reach the seat of that faraway intelligence?)

Only the beast's own soundings—
the language of one god speaking to other gods—
penetrated to where I lived.

XI.

I had believed myself reconciled to this life.

XII.

Descent.

XIII.

The beast's heart is silent.

His internal organs lack heat.

His tail no longer undulates through the depths.

We who live within his corpse are certain of his death.

XIV.

The operations of the body: the lungs drawing air into the warm capillaries of the flesh, the heart's boom, the rush and ebb of the digestive juices had isolated me.

Now I hear others.

Some declare we should share his fate.
Some contend we should shove our way out through the entrails.

I am glad not to see these speakers, these argumentative squeeze boxes, limbs bleached white, faces raw from the acid in the beast.

Les blancs débarquent. Le canon! Il faut se soumettre au baptême, s'habiller, travailler.

They debate the possibility of existence outside our present existence.

If we can survive without the life of the one who gave us life, must we conclude that he was not responsible for our lives?

Perhaps, our words are attempts to measure the beast.

Perhaps, we exist in a series of beasts.

XV.

A sturdy rib, an organ, or muscle offering some worth to this magnificent system: I would have preferred complete incorporation into the beast rather than this disengagement.

Oui, l'heure nouvelle est au moins très sévère.

As a series of cells linked into tissue, I might have traveled the almost infinite space of the oceans for a century.

XVI.

Sunlight, like the fingers of the doubting Thomas, has poked through the beast's wounds.

I have resolved to enter the lungs and exit as a spume through the blowhole.

His frame may stretch across the floor of a shallow sea.

If so, I depart only to drown.

Even if I arrive on a pleasant beach where tourists snap pictures of themselves posing beside the carcass of Leviathan, the return of my senses may prove overwhelming.

Although I push forward head-first into this necessary emergence,

I say to the body I loved:

I leave you unwillingly.

Chris Bullard is a native of Jacksonville, FL. He lives in Collingswood, N.J. He received his BA from the University of Pennsylvania and his MFA from Wilkes University. Plan B Press published his chapbook, *You Must Not Know Too Much*, in 2009. Big Table Publishing published his chapbook, *O Brilliant Kids*, in 2011. WordTech Editions published his first full length book of poetry, *Back*, in November of 2013 his second full-length book, *Grand Canyon*, in 2015. Kattywompus Press published his chapbook, *Dear Leatherface*, in January of 2014 and has accepted his chapbook, *High Pulp*, for publication in 2016. His work has appeared in publications such as *32 Poems*, *Rattle*, *Pleiades*, *River Styx* and *Nimrod*.

www.ingramcontent.com/pod-product-compliance
Lightning Source LLC
Chambersburg PA
CBHW060226050426
42446CB00013B/3183